If you have a home computer with Internet access you may:

- request an item to be placed on hold.
- renew an item that is not overdue or on hold.
- view titles and due dates checked out on your card.
- view and/or pay your outstanding fines online (over $5).

To view your patron record from your home computer click on Patchogue-Medford Library's homepage: www.pmlib.org

WEDDING
HAIKU

WEDDING
HAIKU

Three Short Lines for Your
Two Important Words

EUGÉNIE OLSON

Illustrations by
Nelle Davis

life

Guilford, Connecticut

An imprint of Globe Pequot Press

gpp®
life

GPP Life is an imprint of Globe Pequot Press.

Text design by Sheryl P. Kober
Illustrations by Nelle Davis © Morris Book Publishing, LLC

Library of Congress Cataloging-in-Publication Data
Olson, Eugénie Seifer.
  Wedding haiku : three short lines for your two important words / Eugénie
Olson.
     p. cm.
  ISBN 978-0-7627-4947-8
  1. Haiku, American. I. Title.
  PS3615.L74W43 2009
  811'.6—dc22

2009029534

Printed in China

10 9 8 7 6 5 4 3 2 1

Foreword

"We're engaged!" Is there any other phrase that makes people feel quite so giddy, so proud, so excited? And, truly, is there any other phrase that can drive a normally sane woman to debate over canapés, have dreams about dyed-to-match shoes, fight with friends about dresses, or gamely wear a gigantic hat made of a paper plate and bows?

A wedding is a union between two people who love one another, sure, but every bride-to-be knows that it also means dealing with fussy bridesmaids. It's signing the contract with the DJ, hoping against hope that he won't ask Grandma to rap. It's turning a bridal gown's price tag over and having to lean against a nearby piece of furniture for support.

A girl who's getting married needs some laughs, and she needs them in a hurry.

This is why I created *Wedding Haiku*. In between your trips to the post office and caterer, during your wait for the photographer or your future mother-in-law, steal a moment for yourself and take in a few haiku. I hope you enjoy them, and that they help make quick work of the torturous months between "Yes" and "I do"!

Haiku: A History and How-to

Haiku is an ancient form of Japanese poetry that is 3 lines long and contains 17 syllables. The first line has 5 syllables; the second line has 7; the third has 5. Haiku were traditionally about nature, and the goal was to capture a mood or feeling that would lead the reader to a spiritual revelation or insight.

You undoubtedly have had many moods and feelings about everything that's happened during your engagement—so why not try out a haiku of your own? Just remember to follow the 5-7-5 format and to have your haiku evoke real feelings, whether they're concerns about the cake or worries about how to go to the bathroom in that gown. Have fun, and happy haiku!

Did you see my ring?
I'll just casually sit
with my hand right **here**

Parents' first meeting:
So awkward for all. Can we
get some wine pronto?

❧

Mexican standoff
during reception hall tour
Three brides, two rooms. Gulp.

The wedding planner
sure does seem eccentric, but
they say she's the best!

One bridesmaid's six-two,
One's pregnant, and one's fifteen
Where does a bride start?

Should I change my name?
Well, sure; I love you, honey
just not your last name

shelley Butts
shelley butts
shelley
S. b.
Shelley Butts
Butts
But..

Bridal magazine
features blond, smiling size twos
We must beat them up

Am I wearing white?
Well ... of course I am, Grandpa
Now why wouldn't I?

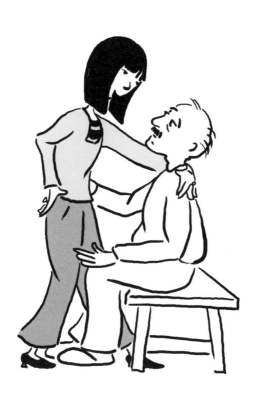

I don't think prenup
needs to include your "special"
chair and ottoman

DJ promises
Def Leppard and lots of Ratt
Uh, we'll be in touch

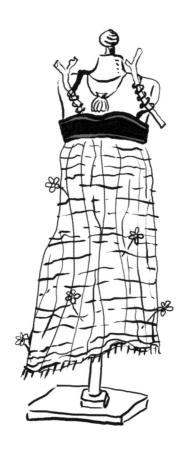

Think again, bridesmaid!
There will be no hemp dresses
"Eco-chic" or not

Cups! Saucers! Napkins!
And such gorgeous silverware!
Baby? Don't you think?

Mom-in-law e-mails:
"Wouldn't lutes be just perfect?"
Can I hit "delete"?

Strapless gown beckons
but thought of thousand arm curls
sends bride scurrying

This is quite a train
I think I see Business Class
and the Café Car

Yes, of course we need
demitasse cups and saucers
What are you, crazy?

Wait just a minute
This price surely includes a
decent used car, right?

Hippie sis requests
vegan cake with soy frosting
I'll get right on that

First bride in my way
gets an elbow in the face
at the one-day sale

Yes, I have seen hell
and it comes in the form of
this bridal boot camp

Oh, what a headache
Running off to Vegas looks
pretty good right now

Do you have one that
doesn't make my butt look like
nuclear meringue?

Champagne? Ivory?
Napkin color is **crucial**
Come on, quit laughing!

Hon, who put these clubs
on our wedding registry?
Any idea?

Does this bustle come
with engineering drawings
or a manual?

I know you love him
But no, Mr. Clyde cannot
be our ring bearer

Wedding dance lessons
end with six pulled muscles and
a mild concussion

Hawaii or Greece?!
With our budget, maybe just
a trip to the shore

I must add this clause:
If I hear "YMCA"
none of you get paid

A Hummer limo?
It's a wedding, hon, not an
Army maneuver

Need to pare down list
Are you sure we need to have
all your frat brothers?

Most beautiful words
for feuding families and
friends: It's Open Bar

Twenty-three things done
Only seventy-four left
I love you, sweet list!

Oh, fussy bridesmaid
I **know** you don't like the shoes
You've told me six times!

Hey, Mr. Postman!
Two-hundred-two invites for
us to hand cancel!

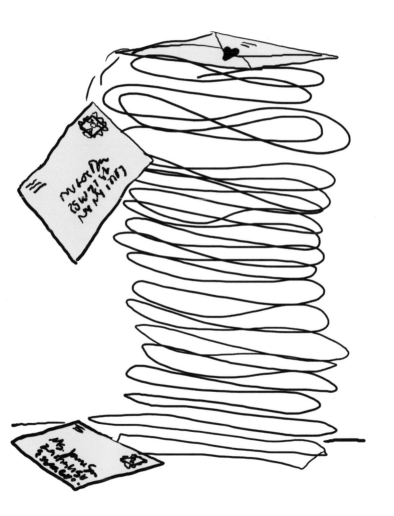

Bridal bingo game—
Such fierce competition for
a plastic spoon rest

Whoops! Tooth whitening
was such a smashing success
fiancé needs shades

Groom's flashy great-aunt
plans to wear pink sequined suit
right in the front row

Fake smile is cracking
under weight of third set of
knitted potholders

Oh, so many bows
Who invented this hat thing,
and can I smack her?

Bakery beckons
to hungry, dieting bride
Must call seamstress, fast

No, I **don't** think that
Hooters gift certificates
make good groomsmen's gifts

Oh, wow, thanks so much!
I always wanted one of . . .
(What the hell is this?!)

Omigosh, Grandma!
This peek-a-boo peignoir set
is making me blush

Had that dream again:
Cake was huge, groom was a bear
and my gown was blue

Yes, it's quite a dress
I've always wanted my own
couture Charmin gown

One more wedding show
and fiancé threatens to
block Lifetime network

Never thought I'd be
so psyched about a blender
and yet here I am!

Yes, this bustier
sure holds in my waist ... is it
getting dark in here?

Wedding cake tasting
ends with manic sugar high
and frosting on face

So many invites
and so few RSVPs
Get with it, slowpokes!

Arugula? Bibb?
Or maybe radicchio?
Oh, such salad stress

Damn you, puberty!
Flower girl has suddenly
gotten her boobies

Get me my cell, stat!
The beverage napkins have
the groom's name spelled wrong!

You are kidding me!
I'm starting my period
on our honeymoon?!

Daddy, why don't **you**
pick the music for our dance?
ABBA? Are you sure?

Little hot glue gun
Are you as sick as I am
of making these things?

Groom's prelim draft of
vows includes reference to
the Boston Red Sox

One more argument
and I *swear* I'm calling the
Jerry Springer Show

Oh, no! B-list guest
asks where invitation is
Ummm … I guess it's lost!?

We can't seat your aunt
near the bar! Remember at
your sister's wedding?

Bachelorette weekend:
Too many cocktails and then
it's bridesmaid mayhem

Honeymoon to Greece
Begins in just sixteen days
Where is your passport?

Oh, I'm **sure** that your
bachelor party was very
quiet and boring

Wait just a minute!
What cop carries a boom box?
Oh, no! Oh, no! Nooo!

Bachelorette party
ends with bride passed out in street
and cameras galore

Of course I love you
But I am not wearing **that**
on our honeymoon!

Oh, boy, lucky me!
My bachelorette party has
such classy items

How many more bags?
One more Jordan almond and
I think I'll flip out

One week 'til The Day
And you decided to get
this haircut from hell?

Last tanning session
may have been one too many
for super-bronzed bride

Pre-honeymoon wax:
If only they made the men
do this sort of thing!

My final fitting!
I've lost weight? Are you for real?
Shout HALLELUJAH!

No rain for six weeks
Now forecast says lots of hail
Stay tuned for tantrum!

Just two days to go
and they want to bring their kids?
I hate your cousins!

Boo ... who planned for the
rehearsal dinner to have
an all-carb menu?

Where is the number
for the dermatologist?
The humanity!

What? We can't throw rice?
What am I going to do
with all of this now?

*If your brother's toast
mentions your former girlfriends
I'm going to scream*

Gasp! Ring bearer put
gigantic piece of chewed gum
in flower girl's hair

Can wedding hairstyle
look a little less like a
crazy Cinnabon?

If she shows off her
Strategy to catch bouquet
one more time, I'll freak

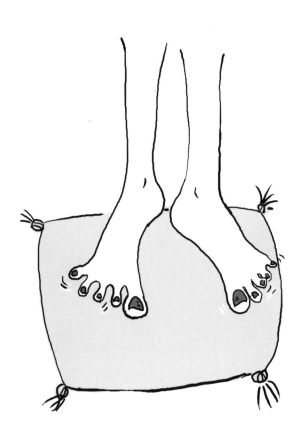

Who says "something blue"
can't be hidden away on
my super-cute toes?

Makeup artist has
very strong opinions on
wedding day eyebrows

Must dispatch groomsman
Aunt Janie and Uncle Stu
missed bus from airport

Be careful with that!
Hairstylist told me it's a
load-bearing barrette

Here, pretty kitty
Just back away from the dress
before I lose it

Busted! Sources say
groom was spotted this morning,
getting his nails buffed

Next problem on list:
How to cover my brother's
Sonic Youth tattoos

Gesundheit! Who knew
his sister was allergic
to calla lilies?

How could I think that
Coming here in your Mini
Was a good idea?

Wedding day cold snap!
Fifty in June—now I have
literal cold feet

Is everyone here?
What do you mean, a groomsman
is stuck in traffic?!

Looks like there will be
uninvited guests at our
lovely beach wedding

Bridesmaid's hung over?
Rehearsal dinner excess?
Tough! Snap out of it!

Who's bringing the rings?
Somebody named "Crazy Carl?"
Just forget I asked

First one who signs our
guestbook with "I.P. Freely"
is gonna get it

Candid shots are fine—
just not of my underwear
and my strapless bra!

Pantyhose on? Check.
Gown zipped? Check. Train fluffed nicely?
And . . . now I must pee.

Veil down, bouquet up
The big day is really here
Time to get married!

Acknowledgments

Special thanks to my agent, Stacey Glick, and to my editor, Mary Norris. As always, huge thank-yous to my family: Les and Amy Seifer, John and Julie Cargill, Ben Seifer, Paul Olson, Nancy Olson, and Susan and Scott Allison; and big smooches to David and Dash.

About the Author

Eugénie Olson is the author of three novels, including *Babe in Toyland*, *The Pajama Game*, and *Love in the Time of Taffeta*. She lives in Somerville, Massachusetts, with her husband and young son, and their two cats.